T0065695

Be A Pebble-Ripples Will Flow

FRESH INSPIRATIONAL INSIGHTS

Lois Stromberg

WESTBOW
PRESS®
A DIVISION OF THOMAS NELSON
& ZONDERVAN

WestBow Press books may be ordered through booksellers or by contacting:

WestBow Press
A Division of Thomas Nelson & Zondervan
1663 Liberty Drive
Bloomington, IN 47403
www.westbowpress.com
844-714-3454

ISBN: 978-1-6642-9211-6 (sc)
ISBN: 978-1-6642-9213-0 (hc)
ISBN: 978-1-6642-9212-3 (e)

Library of Congress Control Number: 2023902412

Print information available on the last page.

WestBow Press rev. date: 02/24/2023

CONTENTS

Note From The Author

Throughout years of reading and meditating on God's word, I have been blessed with some fresh inspirational insights, too exhilarating not to share. As you discover their freshness in this collection of writings, it is my prayer that you will be richly blessed with opportunities to pass them along to others. As *others* remember conversations, they may even become a part of your own legacy that you will leave behind. Just be a pebble. You never know how far the ripples will flow.

INTRODUCTION

Have you ever been reading God's word and suddenly saw something that you had not seen before, even though you had read those scriptures, perhaps many times? If you have ever experienced the thrill of God shedding light on what you just read, and you could hardly wait to share it with others, then you have at least an idea of what this book is about. I became a believer and a devoted reader of the Bible when I was a senior in high school, but it was only after retirement from my teaching career that I began spending more time to read God's word and, perhaps more importantly, to meditate on what I was reading. When God gives fresh inspirational insights to scriptures, it is more exciting than I can narrate. God's purpose for me is to pass along the words He has given me, and so you will find them in the pages of this book. Enjoy and be blessed!

1

GOD'S OBITUARY NOTICE

When a loved one dies, customarily an immediate obituary announcement is made by way of newspapers, social media, personal phone calls, and so forth. Family members and close friends have an urgent desire to get the word out that their loved one has passed away.

But what about God? Surely He made an obituary announcement regarding the death of His Son. God was there when His Son willingly suffered a cruel death on a cross for the sins of all humanity. God, who created the universe—did it matter to Him if or when there would be an obituary about His Son's death? It mattered.

Even so, in my thinking, it stands to reason that God must have reminisced about how He had fellowshipped with Adam and Eve. He created them for His pleasure and enjoyed walks with them in the garden that He had prepared for them. He wanted to have people of His own to love and to be loved by them. But He could not remember the joy they had brought Him without remembering the sin that had caused an immediate separation. He may have reflected on the many generations that had brought Him grief. He knew that because of sin, a sacrifice would have to be made to restore fellowship with humankind. God is holy, and no amount of blood from sacrificed animals could ever pay the full penalty for the sins of the fallen human race. It would take an innocent, sinless human being to make that sacrifice. But there was no sinless human being.

God was well aware that there was only One who could become that sinless human being—God's Son. In times of my own meditation, I have wondered if God considered the depth of evilness of the fallen human race and pondered whether or not they were really worth it—worth sacrificing His Son. If and only if God pondered that question, His next thoughts may have been on a man whom we know as Abraham. Even though Abraham was part of our sinful human race, he showed an unshakeable faith in God through his obedience. If God pondered whether or not humans were really worth it, He may have weighed in with the thought, *Is there even one human being who would do the same for me?*

My thoughts go on to recall God telling Abraham to take his son and offer him as a sacrifice. There is no record of Abraham questioning God, which might seem shocking, but he believed with all his heart that God would keep His promise—his descendants would come through Isaac (See Genesis 21:12). That promise is affirmed in Hebrews 11:18–19, where we also find that Abraham believed God was able to raise Isaac, even from the dead.

When Abraham put his son on the altar and raised his arm with knife in hand, God stopped him. While witnessing the trust that this human being had in Him, perhaps He thought, *They are worth it.* At an appointed time, God sacrificed His Son to provide the opportunity for restoration of the fellowship that was between God and humankind.

Many years went by and animal sacrifices continued, but it was never enough to blot out sin. At last, God had had enough. He sent an angel to tell a virgin named Mary that she had been chosen to give birth to a child who would be the Son of God. It would not be by human conception as we know it, but by the Spirit. God is Spirit. It must have been grief unimaginable to know the cruelty that His Son would suffer from humankind. But it must also have been joy knowing that at last there would be no more sacrifices of animals for sin, which was only temporary and never enough. The ultimate sacrifice of His Son's blood would be enough!

And so we know that while on the cross, God's Son breathed His last breath and uttered the words, "It is finished" (John 19:30). Wham! God sent an immediate announcement, not to the press but to the world. The veil in the Temple was split in two from top to bottom, and God shook the earth; even rocks split. Wow! That was God's obituary notice of His Son's sacrificial death. Never had there been an obituary notice like that one. I wonder if God wept at length over the cruel crucifixion or if His heart danced for joy while waiting for His Son to rise from the grave. It's Friday, but Sunday's coming!

Still, God was not finished with His obituary. We have the official published notice, which includes quite a record of His Son. We call Him Jesus. God also called Him Emmanuel, which means, God with us. This published record includes all that led up to His sacrifice on the cross, His rising from the grave, the forty days He walked among humankind after He arose, His ascension, and His being seated at God's right hand as an advocate for us. It also includes how we can know Him, have fellowship with Him, and be with Him throughout eternity. It is quite a write-up, and it is all included in the book that we know as the Holy Bible.

2

TEAMWORK ON A HOUSETOP

(SEE MARK 2:1–12)

The second chapter of Mark begins by telling us that Jesus was back in Capernaum speaking to people who were crowded into a room, and there was no more room to enter. Outside, four men had brought a paralytic to Jesus, but they were not able to enter the house because of the crowd. The men's perseverance may have been all that parents and perhaps others had instilled in them. Their actions exemplified where there was a will, there was a way.

I propose that they looked at the house, sized up the situation, and glanced up at the roof. Perhaps nodding to each other, they proceeded to climb on top of the house and remove a portion of the roof. That was no small act. For them to take such a bold action, they apparently believed that if they could just get their paralyzed friend to Jesus, he would be healed. They were probably young men who were physically able to climb on top of the house and lift the pallet that carried their paralytic friend. Those four men appeared to have amazing faith. But what about the physically challenged man? He probably also had great faith, but because he was paralyzed and dependent on others, he was likely more reserved than outspoken. Although desperate to be healed, he may have experienced guilt and remorse about damaging someone else's property and being lowered into the middle of a crowd that had just witnessed the whole incident.

The most beautiful part of this story is Jesus's immediate response regarding the guilt and remorse that this young man must also have been feeling for sins that he had committed over a lifetime. The crowd may have wondered if Jesus even noticed that the man was paralyzed because His first words were, "My son, your sins are forgiven" (Mark 2:5). They may have wondered if he had been paralyzed because he had sinned. If so, why wasn't everyone paralyzed? They had all sinned. But these were comforting words to the distraught young man who was lying helpless before Jesus. His sins (plural) were forgiven. What a load was lifted from him. What joy he felt—something like I felt when on one Sunday night in a small neighborhood church, I knelt with a repentant heart before Jesus, and my sins were forgiven.

But there were some informed officials (scribes) who were familiar with the Law. They immediately began to reason that Jesus was blaspheming because according to the Law, only God could forgive sins. Aware in His spirit that they reasoned He was also going to heal the paralytic, Jesus asked them why they were reasoning that way. No record was made that they responded. Jesus tossed them a question to think about: "Which is easier to say to the paralytic, 'Your sins are forgiven'; or to say, 'Arise, and take up your pallet and walk'?" Still, there was no response. He continued, "But in order that you may know that the Son of Man has authority on earth to forgive sins," He said, addressing the paralytic, "I say to you, rise, take up your pallet and go home" (Mark 2:9-11). I can almost see the beaming smile on the young man's face as he acknowledged Jesus's words, picked up his pallet, and walked out as everyone watched.

They were all amazed and glorified God saying that they had never seen anything like that. Those who were present that day had witnessed a never-to-be-forgotten miracle. Surely upon reflection, they recalled that Jesus's first concern had been spiritual, even before the obvious physical need.

Heavenly Father, thank You for caring about all our needs, and help us to remember that Your foremost concern will always be spiritual.

3

DID JESUS MAKE A GRAMMATICAL ERROR?

Before the healing of the leper (recorded in Matthew 8:1–4) and while in Galilee, Jesus had been teaching, proclaiming the gospel of the kingdom, and healing people of diseases and all kinds of sicknesses. Word spread, and "great multitudes followed Him from Galilee and Decapolis and Jerusalem and Judea and from beyond the Jordan" (Matthew 4:23–25). Aware of the multitudes of people, He went up on a mountain and sat down. His disciples followed. What He taught was recorded in three chapters—Matthew 5, 6, and 7. We know it as the Sermon on the Mount. The multitudes remained and were amazed at His teaching. With that as a background, we read the following passage.

And when He had come down from the mountain, great multitudes followed Him. And behold, a leper came to Him, and bowed down to Him, saying, "Lord, if You are willing, You can make me clean." And He stretched out His hand and touched him, saying, "I am willing; be cleansed." And immediately his leprosy was cleansed. And Jesus said to Him, "See that you tell no one; but go, show yourself to the priest, and present the offering that Moses commanded, for a testimony to them." (Matthew 8:1–4)

Jesus had spoken for a long time, and he was once again in the company of that multitude of people. Because of this, He must have experienced fatigue when He came down from the mountain. Nevertheless, He felt compassion and perhaps a renewed energy as he discerned the exceptional faith of the man who had leprosy and said to Him, "Lord, if You are willing, You can make me clean." I can almost see the tender look in Jesus's eyes and hear a compassionate whisper as He leaned closer to the man and replied, "I am willing; be cleansed." I can also visualize the reaction of those in the crowd who were close enough to witness the miracle. They must have responded with demonstrative awe. Some of the people might have pushed others aside to get a closer look. If word spread among the great multitudes of people, there would have been more pushing and shoving to get to the Teacher who taught with authority and miraculously healed a man of leprosy. So

Jesus told the man not to tell anyone but to go and show himself to the priest.

I questioned why Jesus told the man to go show himself to the priest and to present the offering that Moses commanded for a testimony. Upon reflection, I understood that the offering had a purpose. There was a reason for approaching the priest. But more importantly, telling the priest about it and having him personally verify the miraculous healing presented an opportunity for the priest not only to hear but also to believe that Jesus was truly the Messiah. I believe that the man who had just been healed of leprosy slipped away in gratitude. He could hardly wait to show the priest and tell him all about Jesus.

But why did Jesus tell the man to show himself to *the priest* (singular) and present an offering for a testimony to *them* (plural)? Did Jesus make a grammatical error? No way! The offering and the testimony to the priest may have remained singular—one priest. But there were other priests (See Exodus 28:40–41), and the first priest would talk with the other priests. He would tell them what he had seen with his own eyes and heard with his own ears—how Jesus had healed the man of leprosy. Therefore, through one act of obedience, one man was instrumental in spreading the gospel to one priest. In turn, one priest would tell other priests, who would be enlightened. Like a pebble tossed into water, who knew how far that ripple would spread.

How will you handle an opportunity that God sends your way? Sometimes, it is only your presence, a smile, or a spoken or written word of encouragement. Be a pebble. You never know how far the ripples will flow.

4

WEATHER REPORT: FIERCE WINDS

Before the weather changed due to an approaching storm, Mark 4:1–2 (NKJV) tells us that Jesus was teaching by the sea when a great multitude gathered. It was so great that He got into a boat, went out in the water, and sat down. As the crowd listened from the seashore, Jesus began teaching many things through parables. Mark 4:26–29 (NKJV) is my favorite parable that He taught that day. He told them that the kingdom of God is like a man who scattered seed on the ground, but the man did not make it grow. He went to bed at night, got up in the morning, and found that the seeds had sprouted and grown. But how, the man did not know. The soil produced crops by itself—first the blade, then the head, and then the mature grain. When the crops had grown and the grain had ripened, it was then time to harvest them.

I think we may sometimes plant seeds without being aware of it. It may be that as we pass by and speak to others, we share the gospel with someone. Like the planter in the parable, we don't make it grow, but it grows. How does it grow? We may never know, but God knows. It would be wonderful to find out in "harvest-time" that we were the ones who planted the seed.

Moving on to Mark 4:35–41 (NKJV), we find that the multitude continued to crowd the seashore, so when evening came, Jesus said, "Let us cross over to the other side." That was the defining moment of what His disciples would soon experience. They took Jesus in a boat, along with other boats, and set out to cross the sea. After teaching great crowds that day, Jesus rested his head on a pillow in the back of the boat. Soon, the sound of the waves was no longer the peaceful sound that they had heard earlier in the day. Fierce winds arose, and the waves became so high that they were breaking into the boat. There was so much water that they couldn't bail it all out, and the boat was filling up. No, this was not a parable. This was a real-life experience, and fear gripped them.

They looked for Jesus and found Him sleeping, through it all, in the stern of the boat. They woke and asked Him if He cared that they were about to perish. Immediately, Jesus got up, rebuked the wind, and then said to the sea, "Peace, be still."

The wind ceased its blowing, and the sea became perfectly calm. As amazed as they were, Jesus made a crucial point in the form of two questions: "Why are you so fearful?" and "How is it that you have no faith?" I don't think the disciples had answers to those questions. I wouldn't have an answer.

I don't perceive that Jesus asked those questions in a scolding tone. I believe He spoke with great compassion. With their own eyes, they had witnessed His many miracles, yet their attention became so focused on the fierceness of the storm that they didn't seem to remember the events of that day. They were so human (like me). I sense that Jesus had a very compassionate tone as He asked those two questions.

Have you ever been in a spiritual storm where it seemed that Jesus was not aware or tuned into the urgency that you felt? Did you wonder if He was interested or cared about the foreboding situations in your life? It's confession time. I have. More than once, fear has gripped my heart. Sometimes, I feel the winds of an approaching storm, and sometimes, I have no warning. Even though I continue to grow in the Word and have fellowship with the Lord, figuratively speaking, it is not unlike me to try bailing water out of the boat by myself. Eventually, I realize that is not working and that I must boldly run to the One who can speak peace even in the midst of the storm. *Trust* is a word that is synonymous with faith, and peace follows.

Although it may have been a terrible experience, which God did not bring about, whether soon or later after the storm, I often recognize where He made good come out of what was not good. Each storm varies in its force, but they all have the same name: opportunity. Each one is an opportunity to learn and trust Him more. It is followed by a new depth of peace, which comes in no other way.

Dear Lord, in the event of future storms, help me to remember that they are opportunities to trust You more and better enable me to comfort others who might be in the midst of their own fierce winds.

5

IS "LIFE'S PURPOSE" AUTHENTIC?

I don't believe that my parents planned on my birth. My dad's health had taken a turn for the worse and after an extended illness, he passed away, leaving my mother with five older children and a twenty-one-month-old toddler—me. Because of quite a large span of years between my siblings and me, we did not have the same kind of close interaction compared to others who had siblings near their own age. It didn't take much to observe that outsiders saw me as a hardship for the family, and I became aware of that at a very young age.

Throughout my childhood and on into adulthood, I did not understand feelings about my life and the way that I fit in. I certainly could not express them. But one day, I had an experience that changed all of that. It happened on a Labor Day quite some years ago. All was quiet, and I had settled down with a book. The author suggested that I (the reader) think of my heart as a garden and the Lord as the Gardener and then prayerfully consider what the Gardener needed to attend to. I felt impressed to do that, and I did. I don't think I expected anything to happen or at best, I thought I might see a mud puddle instead of a garden. But although my eyes were closed, God showed me how He sees the garden of my heart. It was so real that I dropped down on my knees as tears of joy bathed my face.

When I got off my knees, I went to my computer. With no hesitation or premeditation, my fingers seemed to fly across the keyboard. I am far from being a poet, and the guidelines for poetry may not be consistent, but the result was an autobiographical poem written in third person. It may have been too painful to write in first person. Although I was born on a hot summer day in July, metaphorically, my birth was the onset of the "winter" of my life.

Onset of Life's Winter

The child was born in the onset of winter
Like a tender new rosebud without hope in the winter.
Illness and grief hovered o'er day and night.
No joyous celebrations, only questions of why.

Why, with a dying father and a mother tired and weak,
Would a child be born to add to their grief?
There was hardly enough food for the family to eat,
And now this child—another mouth to feed.

So, a shroud of loneliness she wore as a girl,
Quiet, subdued, distrusting the world.
She felt everyone knew she did not belong,
A burden to the family since her father was gone.

Her brothers and sisters, much older than she,
Shouldered the heavy load of responsibility.
Times were hard, and their sacrifice great.
She perceived a debt she could never repay.

And then one day quite late in her life,
After countless hurts and many a strife,
God showed her a garden with hues so bright
And how He sees her heart in the garden of life.

Tears bathed her face; she sobbed quietly in awe.
She questioned the Lord, then He revealed it all,
How she was entrapped from the moment of birth
And the whys of perplexity she experienced on earth.

He told her He loved her and would do it again—
Choose for her to be born, even in the state things were in.
Drawing her close, as though she sat by His side,
He gave her joy and something akin to pride.

The kind of pride that God must feel
As He looks on her smile and watches her kneel
To worship, praise, and thank Him again
For revealing to her that she is lovely to Him.

Is there a purpose for my life? That is a question often asked by many. Often, the answer is not clear. But God has that answer. There can be no doubt that as unique as we are, God has given us not only life but also a God-given purpose for our lives. In time, I began to see that I had been living God's purpose for me all along. Nothing else could have comforted my mother like their young child that she could hold in her arms and love and be loved, now that her husband was gone. My very presence required hours of attentiveness that could have been only hours of grief. She watched me grow and eventually have a family which brought her joy. When she was advanced in years, I was there for her. Yes, God planned it all before I was born.

Dear reader, your life was well planned before you were born. Long before you graced this earth with your presence, the days that God ordained for you were written in His book. The word *ordained* sounds as though, way back then, you were given a purpose for your life. Ask God to show you that purpose, and you will begin to understand that what you may have considered to be happenstance or circumstance is a manifold connection to the purpose that God has given you. Yes, life's purpose is authentic. And so, dear reader, without exception, as sure as you have life, you have a God-given purpose for your life.

For Thou didst form my inward parts; Thou didst weave me

in my mother's womb. I will give thanks to Thee, for I am fearfully and wonderfully made; wonderful are Thy works, and my soul knows it very well. My frame was not hidden from Thee when I was made in secret, and skillfully wrought in the depths of the earth. Thine eyes have seen my unformed substance; and in Thy book they were all written, the days that were ordained for me, when as yet there was not one of them. (Psalm 139:13–16)

6

DOES MY LIFE EXEMPLIFY LOVE TO MY NEIGHBOR?

One early morning while settling down for an easy coffee-and-biscotti breakfast, I opened my Bible, intending to read a chapter before switching into drive and planning my to-do list for the day. Galatians 5 would be my chapter. Sometime later, I realized that I had mentally pulled over and parked on verses 22–23, which say, "But the fruit of the Spirit is love, joy, peace, patience, kindness, goodness, faithfulness, gentleness, and self-control. Against such things there is no law." Interesting, I mused, there are many laws against doing so many things, but no law existed concerning the fruit of the spirit. There was no declaration for being over-the-limit.

Oh, that we would always live in a way that embodies the fruit of the spirit—not as passive but as activated nouns. I made a commitment to do my part. I even printed a list and used bold fonts for two of them. I chose the largest text that would fit on a page. I displayed them in plain view. I memorized them in the order that they were listed, in hopes of exemplifying them as situations presented opportunities. I find that life is full of situations that present opportunities. How about you?

Several days later, I was reading in Matthew where a lawyer was testing Jesus. For some reason, I always think of him as a young lawyer. Anyway, he asked, "Teacher, which is the great commandment in the Law?" Not hesitating, Jesus said to him, "YOU SHALL LOVE THE LORD YOUR GOD WITH ALL YOUR HEART, AND WITH ALL YOUR SOUL, AND WITH ALL YOUR MIND. This is the great and foremost commandment." Then He gave that young lawyer more information than he asked for: "The second is like it. YOU SHALL LOVE YOUR NEIGHBOR AS YOURSELF. On these two commandments depend the whole Law and the Prophets." (Matthew 22:37–40)

Nothing was mentioned about the lawyer's response, but he had plenty to think about. Actually, I did too. I wondered to what extent my life exemplifies my love for the Lord. It only took a glance at the list of fruit of the Spirit to know that

I would always have plenty of room for growth. As I read the list, I asked the Lord to help me grow an orchard.

I turned to Galatians 5:22–23 in my study Bible. At the bottom of the page, I read the following words:

> "The fruit of the Spirit is love," and it is manifested in joy, peace, patience, kindness, goodness, faithfulness, gentleness, and self-control.
>
> (1) Joy is love's strength.
> (2) Peace is love's security.
> (3) Patience is love's endurance.
> (4) Kindness is love's conduct.
> (5) Goodness is love's character.
> (6) Faithfulness is love's confidence.
> (7) Gentleness is love's humility.
> (8) Self-control is love's victory.
>
> Against such things there is no law." (NASB Loyal Laymen Edition, page 1127)

In Romans 13:10 the apostle Paul reminds us that "love does no wrong to a neighbor; love therefore is the fulfillment of the law." As inconceivable as it seems, the fulfillment of the law hangs upon one word. And so we ask ourselves, *Does my life exemplify love to my neighbor?*

Heavenly Father, may my heart be a reservoir of Your love. Give me wisdom so that I can better understand how to respond in appropriate ways that truly exemplify love to my neighbor and for my neighbor—those people whom You place in my life's path.

7

WHAT ARE WE SUPPOSED TO DO DOWN HERE?

Who we are affects what we do. Our relationship with the Lord is not about trying to do the right thing but about falling in love with Him. The extent that we love Him affects who we are and what we do.

When going through some of my son Sam's writings, I found something he wrote when he was a freshman at Texas A&M University. Perhaps only parents who have lost a child would know how much his words meant. He is no longer in this life. Cancer was the prolonged diagnosis. To all who knew him, his life was a reflection of God's love. While reflecting upon a retreat that he had attended during the previous weekend, he made the following note:

I had a quiet time while I was at Lakeview last weekend. I asked God just exactly what he was going to judge us on. I asked just what it was we were supposed to do down here. He said we would be judged according to how well we loved our brother or something to the effect of how much love we gave to our brother. The question was very direct and sincere, and the answer was immediate and very clear.

According to Matthew 22:35–40 (NKJV), which was the Bible he used, the answer Sam received was clearly indicative of verse 39. These were the words that Jesus followed up with when he responded to a lawyer who asked which was the great commandment in the Law. Jesus's answer was, "You shall love the Lord your God with all your heart, with all your soul, and with all your mind. This is the first and great commandment." But Jesus continued, "And the second is like it: You shall love your neighbor as yourself. On these two commandments hang all the Law and the Prophets."

How do we love our brothers and sisters? We begin with the first and great commandment, which is loving God. We love Him more and more as we get to know Him more and more. This affects who we are and what we do. Without trying, we are a friend to our brothers and sisters, enjoy being with them, listen as they pour out their hearts, encourage them, let them know that we are there for them and that we mean it with all our hearts, and follow up if there are any basic needs.

When Sam prayed and asked God directly and sincerely what we were supposed to do down here, he felt the answer was immediate and very clear: We would be judged according to how well we loved our brother or something to the effect of how much love we gave to our brother. The answer was explicitly in agreement with the second great commandment that Jesus taught: Love your neighbor as yourself.

Heavenly Father, impress upon us what it means to love our brothers and sisters as ourselves. As we live out Your first and great commandment, help us not to neglect the importance of also living out Your second great commandment, which is like it.

8

COUNSEL AND INSTRUCTIONS IN THE NIGHT

Occasionally before I go to sleep, my prayer might be, *Lord, I don't want my mind to be dormant while I sleep. I want even my unconscious mind to be in fellowship with you.* I love it when I awake with a song of praise on my mind. I am made aware that fellowship with Him continued even while I slept. What a great way to begin a day!

Moreover, until I became familiar with the words of Psalm 16:7, I had not considered that the Lord would also counsel and instruct me while I was asleep. We desire to follow the leading of the Holy Spirit, but sometimes we hear Him best when we are quiet and at rest. When I am faced with important decisions, my prayer sounds more like this. *Lord, please instruct me, counsel me in the night, and help me to distinguish your thoughts from my thoughts.* Sometimes when I awake in the morning, I promptly sit up in bed, and the first thought that comes to my mind is a clear direction for the important decision that I prayed about before going to sleep. I do not always receive an answer right away, but when I do, it is as authentic as if I had been awake and personally counseled. Furthermore, it is not unusual for the answer to be reinforced during my time of morning devotion.

Sometimes reading scripture that does not immediately speak to us is like pouring a glass of water, leaving it on the counter, and walking away still thirsty. I believe we often do this. The good side is that sometimes we go back to that glass of water and drink until it quenches our thirst.

Indeed, we are privileged to have this kind of fellowship when we believe that He is and that He will do what He has promised.

And without faith it is impossible to please Him, for he who comes to God must believe that he is, and that he is a rewarder of those who seek him. (Hebrews 11:6)

If we do not believe that He is, our prayers are merely words. But if we believe and ask, He will counsel and instruct us even while we are asleep. I can attest that it's just that easy. Believe and ask. Dear reader, if the words in Psalm 16:7 have not already spoken to you, I hope that soon, you can join me and joyfully attest, "Psalm 16:7 is tried and proven."

I will bless the Lord who has counseled me; indeed, my mind instructs me in the night. (Psalm 16:7)

9

CONVERSATION AT THE FENCE

It was Christmas Eve. I carefully packaged a dozen freshly baked brownies and other goodies into a holiday box. Then I called my new neighbor and asked him to meet me at the fence. He smiled and thanked me for the treats, and we chatted briefly. He asked if my family would be coming for Christmas. My answer was, "Yes." He commented that his dad had been there for a visit and had just driven away. I asked where his dad lived. He named a city and state several hours away. My neighbor went on to say that he had been nervous when he had found out that his dad was coming to visit because his dad didn't agree with his lifestyle. But his more positive summary was, "We didn't talk about that subject today, so it worked out OK."

In a brief moment, I caught a glimpse of his childhood

days. For whatever reason, it appeared that he didn't have a close relationship with his father. Among many possible reasons, I wondered if his father had spent quality time with him throughout his growing-up years or if he had been caught up in a lifestyle, either preventable or unpreventable, that left little time for his family. On the other hand, perhaps it was not entirely the father's fault. I wondered if the son had willfully refused to respond to his father's love and parenting. Either way, there obviously weren't many occasions for conversation between the father and son. I made a mental note to pray for that relationship.

A few days later, that brief neighborly chat was brought into my mind as I was reading some things that Jesus said about praying. He said not to use meaningless repetition when praying, "for your Father knows what you need before you ask Him" (Matthew 6:8). Now that is clear evidence of a loving, caring Father who is available and who desires a close relationship with His children. I paused and meditated on what I had just read. Sometimes we need to take time to do that. It paid off in a way that it would not have if I had not taken the time to stop and meditate. More than ever before, it became compellingly obvious that having a close relationship with my heavenly Father depends not on Him but entirely on me. How often and in what way do I approach Him in conversation? No one can deny that He has already done His part. His Word is not shy about letting us know that He desires to hear from us. He is always available, so it is up to me to make quality time for conversation. It's called prayer.

Even as I write these words, I wonder if this loving reminder about the importance of prayer will remain freshly revealed truth. I wonder if I will seize opportunities to frequently have heartfelt prayer conversations with my heavenly Father and enjoy a continually close relationship with Him. I have that choice, and my lifestyle and yours will reflect the choice that we make.

> *But you, when you pray, go into your inner room,*
> *and when you have shut your door, pray to your*
> *Father who is in secret, and your Father who sees*
> *in secret will repay you* (Matthew 6:6).

10

DON'T OVERLOOK JESUS'S SENSE OF HUMOR

(SEE MATTHEW 11:20–30)

What a Teacher! What a sense of humor! I almost missed it. I had been reading a passage in the eleventh chapter of Matthew. Jesus had just finished reprimanding the cities in which most of His miracles had been done because they had not repented. He told them that if the same miracles had occurred in Sodom, Sodom would not have been destroyed. He warned them, saying, "Nevertheless I say to you that it shall be more tolerable for the land of Sodom in the day of Judgment, than for you" (Mathew 11:24). There was no humor in His voice. He was speaking of judgment.

But as He looked across the crowd and saw a beaten-down,

defeated-looking group of individuals, He was reminded of oxen wearing a yoke and struggling to pull a heavy, loaded cart. His next words were, "I praise Thee, O Father, Lord of heaven and earth, that Thou didst hide these things from the wise and intelligent and didst reveal them to babes" (Matthew 11:25).

With that, He began to address those defeated-looking individuals: "Come to Me, all who are weary and heavy-laden, and I will give you rest. Take My yoke upon you, and learn from Me, for I am gentle and humble in heart; and YOU SHALL FIND REST FOR YOUR SOULS. For My yoke is easy, and My load is light" (Matthew 11:28-30). Many times, I had read that passage, and my mom used to quote it from memory, but this time, I saw more than I had seen before and felt a desire to write about it.

I decided to learn more about oxen, so I began reading about them. I discovered that the type of oxen that lived in western Asia, Europe, and northern Africa were aurochs. They were large animals. They measured six feet high at the shoulders. These remarkable creatures disappeared in about the year AD 1627. I came across several drawings. One of them showed the capture of a wild ox. Another showed tamed oxen, one of them bellowing as it was being driven forward by someone who held a rope that was tied to its hind foot. That drawing caused me to see a smile on the face of Jesus as

He compassionately compared those tired and weary people to oxen. The only kind of yoke that the oxen knew was very heavy. The only kind of cart they knew was one that was loaded. Even though the ox that I saw in the drawing was very large, the heavy yoke and the loaded cart were more than that ox wanted to go near.

The mental image of the ox bellowing as it was driven forward must have been the image that Jesus had when He used the analogy of His yoke being easy and His load being light. After all, the people had been living under the Law, which was a cumbersome yoke and a very heavy load—and it was not the answer. The people were seeking an answer. Even though Jesus was and is the answer, many people were as skeptical as the bellowing ox being driven forward to enter into a new yoke, which was the plan of salvation. The cart, which was the Law with its works, was no longer required works, but required faith, and even that faith comes from Him. Yes! His yoke is easy. A yoke does not work for just one. A yoke is for two, and the other carrier in that yoke is Jesus.

Glancing again over the notes I had made and enjoying the fresh new insight, I felt it was well worth the time I had spent (which was most likely a lot more than my readers would guess). But as I leaned back in my chair, personal application set in. In retrospect, I saw myself over the course of time, bellowing and balking as Jesus tightened a rope around my heel when I strayed from His plan for me. It was probably good to remember some of those times, but the part that made me smile was picturing Jesus shaking His head as He called me His little ox.

Or is that you He is calling His little ox? What a Teacher! What a sense of humor! What a Savior!

11

TRUST AND PEACE ON CRUISE CONTROL

As believers, we know that God is love and that God loves us. Nevertheless, one of the most difficult concepts to fully grasp is that His love does not depend on our performance. If it did, He would not have loved and even died for us when we, as sinners, gave no thought or time to Him. Once we grasp His unconditional, unwavering love as truth, trust increasingly becomes our heartfelt response.

Now and then, I enjoy reminiscing on some of my own trust-building experiences. I especially enjoy reliving a time and specific place in my home where I lived most of my adult life and where I was blessed with both joyful and challenging times. During one of those challenging times, my mind was on a very urgent problem concerning a huge responsibility. I was walking across the den toward the hallway when I strongly sensed God's presence. I did not have a dream or vision like Jacob had, but my response was the same, "Surely the Lord is in this place" (Genesis 28:16). I stood still, and although it was not audible, these words came to me: *Trust me. You read about it, you sing about it, and you talk about it. Now live it.* Although I did not hear the words with my ears, they were very clear, and I knew that they were from the Lord.

My thoughts progressed to a deeper meaning of the word *trust*. My immediate response was, *Lord, I trust You.* With that, I knew He was now in charge and He did not need my help. Becoming aware of a pleasant, calming peace that only He could give, I went about taking care of other matters. Without going into greater detail, the enormous responsibility that was about to become an overwhelming problem was taken care of in a surprising and unexpected way. But isn't that the way God always works?

For My thoughts are not your thoughts, neither are your ways My ways, declares the Lord (Isaiah 55:8).

That experience jump-started my learning to truly trust Him in greater measures than before.

Dear readers, my purpose for writing about this experience and its calming peace is to help you find encouragement by verbalizing, "I trust you, Lord." Also, it is my heartfelt desire that you will not only read about, sing about, and talk about trust but that you will be freshly inspired to fully trust Him in every detail of your life and in reality, live it.

May we always be thankful for His goodness and find that when trust flows effortlessly, peace flows on cruise control.

12

WOMAN AT THE WELL—HER STORY

(ALL SCRIPTURES IN QUOTATIONS ARE FROM JOHN 4:3–39)

If the Samaritan woman who met Jesus at the well had kept a journal, I wonder if her entry might have read something like this:

I noticed that on recent mornings, I was getting out of bed more slowly. My joints didn't move as freely as they used to. I took a moment to rub the back of my neck and the strained muscles in my shoulders before beginning my morning ritual and chores for the day. As I prepared breakfast for my new love, I tried to be cheerful and hummed a little tune that we had danced to only a short while before, when we had first met. I tried to detect even a faint smile on his face, but he reminded me that it was getting late and that he was hungry. Silently, I wondered how the novelty of a relationship could lose its glow so soon. I was already feeling the pangs of insecurity in this relationship. After all, having five marriages slip through my fingers would cause anyone to have insecure feelings. But even discounting that track record, I had a physical reminder that I was not the young woman I used to be. The years were beginning to show.

As the morning wore on, I went about my chores. By noon, I needed to take a break but realized I had not been to the well to draw water for the day. I quickly lifted my water jug to my shoulder and headed toward Jacob's Well. I contemplated that no one would be there at that time of day. Others would have gone before the scorching sun reached high noon, so at least, I would not face the curious and judgmental eyes of other villagers.

Reaching the well, I let the bucket down and tugged at the rope to pull it up. I didn't notice that someone was sitting near the well until he spoke. Startled, I turned to see a man who was obviously a Jew. He looked tired. I reasoned that he must have walked a long way since Jews don't live in Samaria, and for that matter, they don't even associate with Samaritans. I think I felt some resentment at the fact that Jews pride themselves on being superior to Samaritans. Yet this Jewish man was asking me for a drink of water. Although

I also felt a bit of sympathy for Him, I just had to remind him, "How is it that you, being a Jew, ask me for a drink since I am a Samaritan woman?"

As surprised as I was to find a Jewish man at the well asking me for a drink, I was far more surprised at his reply to my question. "If you knew the gift of God and who it is that says to you, give me a drink, you would have asked him, and he would have given you living water."

I was silent for a moment before I spoke again. My words rambled on as I asked what he meant by living water and if he thought that was better than the water from Jacob's well. He told me that whoever drinks of the living water would never thirst again.

My mind did not comprehend the meaning of the words, but something within me did. I could feel weariness leave my body, and it was replaced with a rush of energy and a sense of joy that I had never felt before. Urgently, I said, "Sir, give me this water so I will not be thirsty nor come all the way to draw."

A gentle smile replaced the weariness that I had seen on his face, for he knew that with an open heart, I had already believed. I would come to understand the springs of living water. After a pause, he said, "Go, call your husband, and come here."

I knew that I would not bring my live-in partner. I could not say that he was my husband—not to this man—so I replied, "I have no husband."

If I had not already been amazed, what he said next would have completely astonished me. He spoke with compassion, telling me that I had previously had five husbands and that the man I was living with was not my husband. He told me other things about my life, which an ordinary person could not possibly have known. I inquired if he was a prophet, and if so, why he was not in Jerusalem, the place that people say men ought to worship.

I don't remember all the things that he said to me that day, but I do remember him saying, "God is Spirit, and those who worship him must worship him in spirit and truth."

I was trembling as I said to Him, "I know that Messiah who is called Christ is coming. When that one comes, he will declare all things to us."

Then he spoke the words that I shall never forget: "I who speak to you am he."

I don't know what I would have done at that moment if some other men had not come walking up to the well. Apparently, they knew him and started asking him why he was talking to a Samaritan woman. Still feeling this unexplainable surge of energy, I forgot about my water pot and not giving this man the drink of water that he had asked for. Instead, I turned and went back to my home in the city. I walked fast and actually ran part of the way.

I was energized but breathless as I reached the city. I knew

In my heart that I had met the Messiah at the well, but I also knew that as a woman, I should be cautious about how I would break this news to the men. I said what I had been rehearsing along the way: "Come, see a man who told me all the things that I have done; this is not the Christ, is it?" The men were astounded to see this commonplace, not-so-young woman, who was breathless from running and excited with the exuberance of youth. With curiosity, they each gave a nod and headed for the well.

I hardly remember my numerous afternoon chores, but I remember that all was accomplished in remarkable time. Most of all, I remember the peace that I felt and the beginning of my understanding concerning the concept of living water.

That evening, the men returned to the city, along with the water jug. The Messiah—the Christ—came with them. He stayed in the city for two days, and many Samaritans believed in him because I had testified, "He told me all the things I have done."

As she closed her (what if) journal, I believe she may have experienced a first-time feeling that there was a purpose for her life. To Jesus, the importance of a Samaritan woman was no less than the importance of anyone else, and so her legacy lives on.

Dear reader, in the eyes of God, no one is insignificant. God has a purpose for your life, and no one else can fulfill that purpose in the way that you can. Have you thought about what the legacy of your life will be? What statement about your life will you leave behind? May it be that God did something in you and because of that, God did something through you.

13

IN HIS IMAGE

The Bible tells us who God is, but often we read right over it without grasping the awesome concept that He is not a physical being but Spirit. When explaining true worship to the Samaritan woman at Jacob's Well, Jesus said, "God is Spirit." He didn't say that God is *a* Spirit or that God has a Spirit, but God *is* Spirit. Then He went on to explain, "Those who worship Him must worship Him in spirit and truth" (John 4:24).

It might help to remember that God created humankind (us) in His image.

Then God said, "Let us make man in Our image, according to Our likeness." (Genesis 1:26)

Because He created us like Him, it seems reasonable that God sees each of us as spirit with a physical body rather than a physical body with spirit.

God sees not as man sees, for man looks at the outward appearance, but the Lord looks at the heart. (1 Samuel 16:7)

But what about Jesus? He had a physical body.

In the beginning was the Word and the Word was with God and the Word was God ... And the Word became flesh and dwelt among us. (John 1:1, 14)

Colossians 1:15 reminds us, "He is the image of the invisible God, the first-born of all creation." Jesus was God in the flesh during His time on earth. But He is no longer with us on earth.

Now it came to pass, while He blessed them, that He was parted from them and carried up into heaven. (Luke 24:51 NKJV)

But wait! He did not go without leaving a most comforting promise. That promise was to send the Holy Spirit (not flesh again but this time, the Spirit) to live within us.

I will ask the Father, and He will give you another Helper, that He may be with you forever; that is the Spirit of Truth whom the world cannot receive because it does not behold Him or know Him, but you know Him because He abides with you and will be in you. (John 14:16–17)

With that realization, worship can take on a different paradigm. No longer are we required to go to Jerusalem or wait until we are in church to worship. God has made it so easy, and we are privileged to be able to worship God anytime and anywhere—sometimes without speaking, praying aloud, or even whispering. The apostle Paul said, "Pray without ceasing" (1 Thessalonians 5:17). He didn't mean that we should always get away to some private place, get on our knees, and pray on and on without ceasing. No doubt, Paul was worshipping and praying (in spirit and in truth) as he was writing those words.

Dear Father, help us to be mindful that You always see our hearts and that whether we are praying aloud or silently, we should always pray in spirit and in truth. Thank You for giving us the awesome privilege of communicating with You, not only in a specific place of worship or in our homes but wherever we happen to be—any time and any place.

14

NEW CONCEPT OF GOD'S LOVE

I believe that there is a difference between sin and fault. I am not dogmatic about it, and I would not argue its case, but after studying the scriptures over a period of years, in all sincerity, it appears to me that there is a difference between sin and fault. If we know that something is wrong but do it anyway, that is sin. James 4:17 also tells us, "…to one who knows the right thing to do, and does not do it, to him it is sin," Therefore, I believe sin is intentional.

On the other hand, I believe faults are not intentional. We will always have faults because we are human beings. We will never be perfect because we are human. Only God is without fault.

With that being said, I want to share words written by my son, Sam. Even though he passed away several years ago, his new concept of God's love is still being passed along to others, who are then also encouraged. My intent for publishing this book is that you will find refreshing inspirational insights and encouragement and then pass them along to encourage others, who perhaps will continue to do the same. I found the words Sam had written on a sheet of lined note paper when he was an Aggie freshman. Here are his words, just as he had written them:

> I read part of a Billy Graham book today and was struck by a new concept of God's love. It goes like this: I've failed God and have wandered away from Him several times. I've doubted Him, took Him for granted, and ignored Him on occasion. However, that might not be as bad as it sounds because of what a relationship between two people means. Love basically erases wrong. So having no inclination to terminate my relationship with Christ (though it may suffer from time to time), we can both look at my faults in good faith and realize that though they may be frustrating and not really desirable, my faults don't have anything to do with my commitment to Christ or His commitment to me. And when I see that I've

missed the boat, I feel a little disgusted. I look at Christ, and we both laugh because I'm so dumb. And He and I both know I really have no desire to hurt Him. I'm human, I'm struggling, but I sure appreciate His understanding and His mercy and His unwavering commitment to me.

Dear reader, be encouraged. God hates sin, but He loves you—faults and all.

15

FRIENDSHIP

Although we lived in a large city, our home was located on a secluded, wooded lot, with more than enough yaupons, tall pines, and spreading oaks. The trees were homes and playgrounds for a myriad of birds and squirrels, due to the seeds that we daily scattered across a portion of our backyard.

Ray, my husband, had been feeding nuts to a particular fox squirrel that became quite friendly. It was during one spring break that I took advantage of spending time on the back patio and decided to pursue a friendship with Ray's little friend. Giving him nuts from my hand, I began coaxing him onto the patio and then into the house. Leaving the patio door open, I filled my hands and pockets with almonds, which we had brought from the West Coast. Little by little, I gained his trust. He ventured through the doorway, into the den, and across the room where I was seated. With each nut I gave him, he would dash out the door, quickly bury it, and return for another. Sitting on the floor, I encouraged him onto my lap for another almond and even let him take some from my pocket (Wisdom must have been taking a break). Twice, he didn't take the time to go outside and bury the almond. He buried them in a nearby shag rug, pulling the pile over the almond as best he could. It was sheer delight for both of us.

That friendship continued for at least four years. At times, it would be several days before we would see him, but he would always look for us when he returned. One day after an extended absence, we were delighted to see him again. Clutching a handful of nuts, we hurried outside. However, our spirited little friend was so anxious that as Ray was handing him a pecan, he grabbed for it, digging his claws into Ray's thumb. It was painful, and the thumb bled a lot. Of course, we continued enjoying his friendship but also knew it was possible that he might hurt us while he focused on satisfying his own needs or desires. From then on, we were more cautious, and we no longer handed him nuts but placed them one at a time on the patio—not quite as intimate, but patios don't bleed. He was still as endearing as when he took almonds from my pocket, but I had been made keenly aware of his nature from birth and that his innate nature would not change.

Some years later, I was reminded of our little friend as I was reading and meditating on the second chapter of John. Jesus had just begun his public ministry. He had gone to the Passover in Jerusalem, cleaned up the monetary corruption that was going on in the Temple, and performed miraculous signs. John 2:23–24 tells us, "Many believed in His name, beholding His signs which He was doing. But Jesus, on His part, was not entrusting Himself to them, for He knew all men." No one has ever loved people more than Jesus, yet because He knew what was in humans, He did not entrust Himself, even to those who believed in Him.

In summary, reflecting on my friendship with the little squirrel led me to think about our human friendships and that they must not be held to a standard of perfection. Like you and me, our friends are also human, and they have innate imperfect natures. With that in mind, let's be encouraged to enjoy the friends that God places along our lives' paths. Love them and let them know we love them and that their friendship is one that we treasure. If we encounter some imperfection, let's chalk it up to their innate natures (due to a fallen world) and keep loving them and being grateful for their friendship, which is one of God's most precious gifts.

16

AND HE WAS RICH

LUKE 19:1–10 NKJV

Then Jesus entered and passed through Jericho. Now behold, there was a man named Zacchaeus who was a chief tax collector, and he was rich. And he sought to see who Jesus was, but could not because of the crowd, for he was of short stature. So he ran ahead and climbed up into a sycamore tree to see Him, for He was going to pass that way. And when Jesus came to the place, He looked up and saw him, and said to him, "Zacchaeus, make haste and come down, for today I must stay at your house." So he made haste and came down, and received Him joyfully. But when they saw it, they all complained, saying, "He has gone to be a guest with a man who is a sinner." Then Zacchaeus stood and said to the Lord, "Look, Lord, I give half of my goods to the poor; and if I have taken anything from anyone by false accusation,

I restore fourfold." And Jesus said to him, "Today salvation has come to this house, because he also is a son of Abraham; for the Son of Man has come to seek and to save that which was lost."

When Jesus walked among the crowds, the average person was not rich (just as it is today). Crowds following him were probably people of average economic status. Some were below average, such as the widow who gave her last coin, those who were paralyzed or blind, and others who had disabilities and could not work. Did this mean that Jesus was not inclusive? No way. The writer made that clear when he pointed out that Zacchaeus was a chief tax collector, and he was rich.

As I was reflecting on the passage about Zacchaeus's determination to see Jesus, I noted that *he was rich*. Yes, he was a chief tax collector, but my eyes drifted back to the words "and he was rich." He was also of short stature. I am not rich, but I am also of short stature. I was attending several services at a large church and was having a difficult time seeing written hymns on a screen because of taller people in front of me. Since there was no tree to climb (as if I would choose to do so), I decided to take the elevator up to the balcony, where I no longer had a problem seeing the words on the screen. Since Zacchaeus had neither an elevator nor a balcony, he just climbed right up a nearby tree. Sure, people were looking, but this man was not inhibited in the least. Although he was not well received as a tax collector, my guess is that he was creative and probably a very likeable person. At any rate, his heart was receptive to Jesus.

Did you notice that Jesus was equally comfortable with the rich as He was with the average or the very poor? He called Zacchaeus personally by name and felt free to invite himself to his house. I find it reasonable to assume that Zacchaeus lived nearby because the crowd followed them and watched as Jesus received a joyful welcome into the rich tax collector's house. On the contrary, the crowd outside did not share Zacchaeus's joyful mood. Overhearing complaints within the crowd that Jesus had gone to be the guest of a man who was a sinner, Zacchaeus was swift to say, "Look, Lord, I give half of my goods to the poor; and if I have taken anything from anyone by false accusation, I restore fourfold." Surely, it was an indication that he did not let the wealth of that world take priority over his life as a believer.

I can only imagine the joy and tremendous peace Zacchaeus must have felt to hear Jesus declare, "Today salvation has come to this house, because he also is a son of Abraham; for the Son of Man came to seek and to save that which was lost."

Yes, Jesus was and is inclusive. He died for all so that all might believe and be saved. From the poorest to the richest to those in between, It Is not a social or economic status but a change of heart that makes the difference.

Command those who are rich in this present age not to be haughty, nor to trust in uncertain riches but in the living God, who gives us richly all things to enjoy. (1 Timothy 6:17–18 NKJV)

17

WAS JESUS'S PRAYER FOR SIMON PETER ANSWERED?

LUKE 22:31–34

"Simon, Simon, behold, Satan has demanded permission to sift you like wheat; but I have prayed for you, that your faith may not fail; and you, when once you have turned again, strengthen your brothers." And he said to Him, "Lord, with You I am ready to go both to prison and to death!" And He said, "I say to you, Peter, the cock will not crow today until you have denied three times that you know Me."

Peter had never known Jesus to be wrong, but surely, Jesus must be mistaken this time. Peter had been loyal to Him for three years. Could Jesus really believe that he would desert Him and deny that he even knew Him?

Jesus was not mistaken. During one of the times when He slipped away to pray, the Father gave Him a heads-up concerning Satan wanting to sift Peter like wheat. Satan did not ask for just any apostle. Oh, no, he most wanted the downfall of Peter. He knew that Jesus had told Peter, "You are Peter, and upon this rock I will build My church; and the gates of Hades shall not overpower it" (Matthew 16:18). The Greek meaning of the name Peter is rock (The *Strongest NASB Exhaustive Concordance*).

After the promised Holy Spirit had come, Peter was the one who preached that remarkable sermon the day the church was born. Many became believers that day.

So then, those who had received his word were baptized; and there were added that day about three-thousand souls. (Acts 2:41)

We can be sure that Satan did not want that to happen. Remember, he even tried to get permission to shake Peter up (sift him like wheat).

Jesus foreknew that Peter would deny that he knew Him. But what did Jesus do? He prayed for Peter. Talk about loyalty! Talk about love! Let's look at what Jesus told Peter about His praying: "That your faith may not fail" (Luke 22:32). Peter was going to deny that he even knew Him. Wouldn't that be a sure sign that his faith had failed? No, because Jesus continued, saying, "And you, when once you have turned again, strengthen your brothers." Jesus knew that Peter unequivocally believed in Him. When Jesus asked his disciples, "Who do you say that I am?" Simon Peter said, "Thou art the Christ, the Son of the living God" (Matthew 16:15–16).

On the night that Jesus was arrested, "Peter also was following Him at a distance as far as the courtyard of the high priest, and entered in, and sat down with the officers to see the outcome" (Matthew 26:58). Peter knew that he was taking a chance by entering the courtyard. He knew that the crowd had seen him with Jesus when they had arrested Him. In fact, Peter, in an attempt to defend Jesus, cut off the right ear of one man in the crowd. That crowd had also gone to the courtyard. Now Peter had reason to fear for his own life, but he wanted to know what was going to happen to Jesus.

From the courtyard, Peter watched as Caiaphas questioned Jesus. Some within the crowd were yelling lies (false witnesses) about Him. He was being mocked. Some began to spit on Him. They blindfolded and beat Him. Satan's unseen presence was in that courtyard, and his plan was to sift Peter like wheat.

When one of the servant girls of the high priest saw Peter warming himself by a fire, she looked at him and said, "'You too, were with Jesus the Nazarene.' But he denied it saying, 'I neither know nor understand what you are talking about.' And he went out onto the porch" (Mark 14:67–68). What were Peter's thoughts? We don't know. He may have thought about leaving because in Matthew 26:71, we find that he was near the gateway: "And when he had gone out to the gateway, another servant-girl saw him and said to those who were there, 'This man was with Jesus of Nazareth.'"

He was not in a safe place, and he knew it. The situation did not look good, and for the second time, he denied knowing Jesus. Nevertheless, those around him were not convinced. Bystanders stepped up, accused Peter of being one of them, and said that they could tell because of the way he talked (He was Galilean). In fear of his life, Peter must have felt trapped with no way out. He began to curse and swear, and for the third time, Peter denied knowing Jesus. Immediately, a cock crowed.

With that abrupt wake-up call, Peter remembered that Jesus had said before the cock crowed, he would deny Jesus three times. I don't believe Satan had considered Peter's next step.

And he went out and wept bitterly. (Matthew 26:75)

Oh, how God loves a repentant heart! Peter's actions had failed miserably, and Peter knew it. Oh, yes, he wept bitterly. However, his faith in Jesus had not failed, and Jesus knew it would not fail. Remember that He had said to Peter, "When once you have turned again, strengthen your brothers" (Luke 22:32). Isn't it interesting that the apostle whose actions appeared weakest of the eleven was the one who was told to strengthen the others? That agrees with other scriptures that tell us how God often works.

We cannot deny Peter's human failure, but there is another thought.

And we know that God causes all things to work together for good to those who love God, to those who are called according to His purpose. (Romans 8:28)

It doesn't say that all things happen for good. It was not good that Peter denied knowing Jesus, but good came out of even that. For one thing, Peter learned what it was like to reach the bottomless pit of regret and to weep unrestrained from a sorrowful heart. Through that experience, he gained an awareness that Satan was waging a battle for people's minds. Consequently, that excruciatingly dreadful experience was invaluable toward his following the instructions that Jesus gave him—to strengthen his brothers. Peter's depth of remorse and repentance made him stronger than he had been before. He was well prepared to receive the Holy Spirit, boldly stand up, and tell it like it was to all within his hearing.

Jesus knew Peter's humanness, and He knows ours. Sometimes we may fail miserably, but He also knows that when our faith is firmly built on Jesus Christ, who is **the Rock**, we are secure in Him for all eternity, and our faith will not fail. May we make it a point to learn from our experiences and look for the good that God will work in and for us.

Here Is my prayer. Dear reader, I invite you to make it yours.

Heavenly Father, help me to live in such a way that others recognize that I am one of Yours. May my words, actions, and lifestyle never, in any way, suggest to others that I don't even know You.

18

HIDDEN
TREASURES

*That their hearts may be encouraged, having been knit together
in love, and attaining to all the wealth that comes from the full
assurance of understanding, resulting in a true knowledge of
God's mystery, that is, Christ Himself, in whom are hidden all the
treasures of wisdom and knowledge.* (Colossians 2:2–3)

One early morning as I was beginning to read the second
chapter of Colossians, the words "God's mystery" became an
attention-getter. God's mystery was Christ Himself. I thought
about it awhile, and yes, Christ and everything about Him
was a mystery that could only be revealed by faith, which
also comes from God. Continuing, a word in verse 3 seemed
to stand out. All the treasures of wisdom and knowledge
are hidden within Christ. Because I had been praying about
wisdom in decision-making, the word *hidden* caused me

to pause again. Wisdom is hidden in Christ, but how do we find it? I remembered the words about prayer that Jesus Himself had spoken: "Ask, and it shall be given to you; seek, and you shall find; knock and it shall be opened to you" (Matthew 7:7).

I find that those words are an acronym and are easy to remember.

Ask
Seek
Knock

Ask, and it shall be given you. Ask for wisdom that is hidden. Where? In Christ. Christ is the source of wisdom.

Seek, and you shall find it. To find it, I must seek its source (Christ), which means spending time with Him—not rushing but waiting and meditating on what I find in His Word.

Knock, and it shall be opened to you. Ask, seek, and knock. Ask but don't stop there. To find wisdom hidden in Christ, we must seek to find it. Seek is not passive. It is more like searching—maybe searching for an address until we find it above a door and then knocking on that door until the door opens. When we visit someone and knock on the door, and it is opened, the next time we visit, we don't expect the door to open because we knocked the last time that we were there. We must knock again.

While continuing to seek, I believe the meaning of the word *knock* is something like *being consistent*. I love going on early morning treasure hunts. I enjoy knowing that many other people throughout the world (in their own time range) are opening their Bibles and going on their own early morning treasure hunts.

Maybe early morning doesn't work for you. Perhaps your best time is during a lunch break, afternoon break, or a quiet time at night. Whatever works is your best time to read God's Word. Take time to watch for hidden treasures that you may have overlooked before. The assurance of fully understanding will encourage your heart and whet your appetite to search for more. The Bible is full of hidden treasures and finding them never gets old. He makes all things new.

19

MANIPULATIVE EIGHT-DAY CLOCK

I listened as I heard the clock striking but apparently miscounted the strikes. An eight-day clock rested on the mantle above my fireplace. It was a gift from my two brothers, as a way of saying thanks for taking care of our mother, especially during the last days of her life. What a lovely gift and one that still reminds me of their love. But that day, the striking sound of the clock took my thoughts in another creative and perhaps fantasized direction.

The key word is *suppose*.

Suppose this eight-day clock, like people, had the ability to make choices. When I set the clock to 10:00, it would decide that two strikes were enough and a better choice than ten. Suppose I kept setting and resetting the clock, but it manipulated the number of strikes it made. Would that make sense? Does it make sense that although God has given me life and purpose, I insist on being in control of my life, even when I know it doesn't match His plans? God is my Creator and rightful owner; therefore, should I, like the imagined manipulative clock, rationalize that I can postpone the timing of something that the Lord clearly directs me to do? A clock doesn't please its owner if it doesn't work as it was designed to work. It is simply taking up space on the mantle.

Sometimes other things seem more urgent, but they are manipulative strikes that distract us from the purpose and timing God has for us. We may have good intentions of getting around to it later, but postponement is not obedience. It is often a lost opportunity.

Lord, search my heart and embed the awareness that You have given me a unique purpose and that I am not here just to take up space. May I remember the importance of acting on Your timing and never neglect an opportunity that You send my way.

20

ONE FOGGY MORNING

On the mornings when I wake up, open my blinds, and find a nice sunshiny day, I enjoy it and tell the Lord that I am grateful for another day. But what about the misty, foggy mornings when I can see no sun?

Recently, I opened my blinds, peered out into a new day, and observed fog hovering as far as I could see. Although it was not unusual, it got my attention in an unusual way. As I stood gazing out that window, the morning fog became a symbolic, spiritual metaphor. With that thought, I desired to be in the fog, so I walked outside and stood on the newly mowed lawn. The air seemed to be clear where I was standing. Only at a distance was the fog distinctly visible. In reality, I knew that I was standing in the midst of it, but fog is not visible at close range. I only knew that it was present where I was because it was present in my observable distance.

I contemplated that as human beings, we are confined to being in only one place at a time. But God is not in human, physical form. God is Spirit, and He has no boundaries. He is always with us. He hears our prayers while at the same time, He hears infinite numbers of prayers coming from the whole world.

While I stood observing fog in a park across the street and beyond it, I did not question how that fog could also be present throughout the entire community. Seemingly, it had no boundaries. Symbolically, the fog gave me a frame of reference to explain God's omnipresence. In no way am I suggesting that the fog was God's presence, but it was a humankind frame of reference that helped enlighten the reality of God's presence.

Since that morning, there have been more foggy mornings. Sometimes while I am opening my blinds and peering out my window, I am reminded of that metaphoric frame of reference. Although I cannot see God, I know that He is with me and all around me. Dear reader, it doesn't take a lot of excitement to make me happy. With a joyful heart, I know that at the same time He is with me, He is with you and all of those who are around us.

The next time you look out into a foggy morning, you

might remember reading this account of my foggy-morning experience. You might briefly wonder if your family members or others are also seeing fog. The fog may or may not be where they are, but you can be sure that the same Spirit of God that is with you is wide enough, high enough, and deep enough to reach your family members and others, wherever they might be.

Be it sunshine, fog, or any other kind of morning, may we always be grateful for His presence with us and all around us and for His precious gift of another day.

21

THE MIRACLE
WE WALK ON

He causes the grass to grow for the cattle, and vegetation for the
labor of man, so that he may bring forth food from the earth.
(Psalm 104:14)

How many times have we read that verse without consciously identifying the miracle that we are reading? Take a little seed, lay it on the kitchen counter or anywhere you wish, and watch to see if you can make it grow. You can talk to it daily, ask it to grow, sing to it, or demand it to grow. Even if it were left there for years or generations, that little seed would not grow.

But take that little seed, put it on the bare ground, cover it with a handful of dirt, and watch what happens. Check on it daily and watch for something green to emerge from the spot where you planted that small seed. Watch it become a plant and watch it grow. You haven't sung to it or told it to grow. What made it grow and eventually produce vegetation? The same earth that we take for granted (and walk on every day) made it grow and produce food. What kind of miracle is that? What kind of miracles do we take for granted every day of our lives?

It is now quite late at night, but when morning comes, I want to walk out on my grassy lawn, run my fingers across the soil of my flower bed, and with all my heart, thank God for the ground that I am standing on—the same earth that He causes to bring forth food. With heartfelt reverence, I want to become more and more mindful of the miraculous details of His creation.

Who would have thought those few words in Psalm 104:14 could be so enlightening? The words are not new to me. I don't know how many times I have read them, but this time, it was as if they suddenly stood up and shouted, *Wait! Look what you just read!* As thoughts began to flow, I reached for my pen and began to write.

Now I begin to wonder what miracles my readers will see for the first time. Some will see spiritual insights that they have previously missed. Some will see new applications that personally relate only to them. Dear reader, whatever yours are, don't lose them. Consider writing about and keeping them with your personal notes or in a journal so that you will not lose those moments of fresh insights that God gives you. Keep reading. It will happen.

The notes you write and those you share in conversation will be intertwined in the legacy that you leave behind. Be a pebble and trust that the ripples will flow far and wide. In this life, we will not know the extent of the ripples, but God knows, and He has a way of directing them. Just be a pebble, and ripples will flow.

22

ANGELS WATCHING OVER US

Second Kings 6 gives an account of a plot to capture Elisha. The king of Syria was making war with Israel. He learned that Elisha, a man of God, was in Dothan and sent horses, chariots, and a great army to surround Dothan.

Now when the attendant of the man of God [Elisha] had risen early and gone out, behold, an army with horses and chariots was circling the city. And his servant said to him, "Alas, my master! What shall we do?" So he answered, "Do not fear, for those who are with us are more than those who are with them." Then Elisha prayed and said "O Lord, I pray, open his eyes that he may see." And the LORD opened the servant's eyes and he saw; and behold, the mountain was full of horses and chariots of fire all around Elisha. (2 Kings 6:15–17)

The angels in charge of protecting Elisha were not physical

men on horses. When Elisha asked God to open the young man's eyes, keep in mind that whatever form the guardian angels appeared to be, they could only be seen when they were spiritually revealed. Angels are spirits, and human eyes are not structured to see spirits.

I wonder if there have been times when angels have appeared in various forms for my protection, and if so, what forms have they been? Perhaps they have been in the form of a truck in front of me, stalled at a railroad crossing. Who knows? I do believe that unseen angels have protected me from danger and at least once, from death. It happened as I was driving home from the post office. The light was green, and I was already out into the middle of the intersection when a speeding black car ran a red light and sped past me. I felt a strong wind swoosh by, and it seemed almost as if the front of my car had been hit. When I got home, I walked to the front of my car and looked at it. Black paint was all across the front of my silver car. When I took it to get an estimate for a new paint job, the technician was able to use a light electric sander and completely remove the black paint. There was no sign of even a dent. I felt strongly that I had been very close to death—as close as that sheer layer of black paint. The words of Psalm 91:11 became more real to me than ever before: "For He will give His angels charge concerning you, to guard you in all your ways."

As we reflect on scriptures where angels appeared in physical forms, the form was appropriate for the occasion. For Elisha, it was men on horses and chariots of fire.

Angels are "ministering spirits, sent out to render service for the sake of those who will inherit salvation" (Hebrews 1:14). Our eyes are not structured to see spirits, but according to scripture, it is possible that angels can also visit us while we remain unaware of it.

Do not neglect to show hospitality to strangers, for by this some have entertained angels without knowing it. (Hebrews 13:2)

This scripture is a comforting assurance that God is our protector and that He takes care of us in various and unexpected ways. May we always acknowledge Him and give thanks for the way that He cares for and watches over us.

23

MARTHA— PENNY FOR YOUR THOUGHTS

Perhaps it is because of our busy lifestyles that I haven't heard, "Penny for your thoughts," in a long time. When someone appears to be lost in deep thought, someone else might say, "Penny for your thoughts," which is a colloquial expression that means, "What are you thinking?" After reading the following passage, I think that if I had been there, I might have looked at Martha and said, "Penny for your thoughts."

> Now as they were traveling along, He entered a certain village; and a woman named Martha welcomed Him into her home. And she had a sister called Mary, who moreover was listening to the Lord's word, seated at His

feet, But Martha was distracted with all her preparations; and she came up to Him, and said, "Lord, do you not care that my sister has left me to do all the serving alone? Then tell her to help me." But the Lord answered and said to her, "Martha, Martha, you are worried and bothered about so many things; but only a few things are necessary, really only one, for Mary has chosen the good part, which shall not be taken away from her." (Luke 10:38–42)

I always felt concerned about Martha when I read that passage. She seemed to be a giving person with a servant's heart. Didn't somebody need to prepare food for all the guests? Was Martha expected to do it alone when her sister was there and could help? One summer day, I was lost in my own reflections about Jesus's words to Martha. Because Jesus said she was worried and bothered about so many things, I wondered what Martha was doing and thinking as she was preparing for her guests. Of course, no one knows what her thoughts were, but I began making an attempt to get to know her by creating a scenario of what might have been her thoughts and actions. The following is that scenario.

Jesus, the Messiah, the One who raised my brother from the dead, is a guest in my home. He is teaching an audience, not in a synagogue but in my house. This is history in the making. Where is that white linen tablecloth? Oh yes, I think it is in the top drawer of the buffet. I will try not to disturb those who are in the living room. Jesus is such an interesting teacher. Martha proceeds to get the tablecloth. *No one even looked up. Let me get Mary's attention. I will motion for her to come and give me a hand.* Martha waves, and Mary looks up, hesitates, and then turns her attention back to Jesus. Martha finds the cloth and returns to the kitchen. She thinks that Mary will follow her shortly.

I need something for a centerpiece. Oh, the roses in my front flower bed are in bloom. I hesitate to cut them. They look so beautiful out front. Oh well, this is a very special occasion and deserves the best.

Taking a small tool for cutting, Martha goes out the back door and walks around to the front flower bed. As she is clipping the rose stems, she catches Mary's eyes again and motions for her. Mary sees her but appears to be caught up in what Jesus is saying. *It doesn't seem to occur to her that she is needed to help prepare not only the food but also all the other things that make a special time for an honored guest.*

Martha returns to the kitchen with the roses. *Honestly, I would like to be sitting down there listening to Jesus, too, but somebody needs to do what I am doing. There! That makes a very attractive centerpiece—roses from my own garden. Oh, my, the pot on the stove is about to boil over. That's all I need.* As she stirs, Martha decides that it is ready to serve.

Oh, the plates! They are in the buffet too. Martha takes the tablecloth into the dining room and spreads it over the table. She stays very busy as she places the vase of roses on the table and sets the stack of plates, silver, glasses, and pitcher of water on the table. *I can't do all this by myself. Mary is going to have to get herself in here and give me a hand. What on earth is she thinking? Obviously, it's not about these people who are going to need something to eat and their impression of us.* Martha walks a little closer, nods, and whispers, "Mary," but Mary doesn't acknowledge that she has heard her. Martha sees that Jesus is aware of her trying to get Mary's attention, but He makes no effort to intervene.

Enough is enough! Mary is going to have to show more responsibility, and as honorable and wonderful as Jesus is, He needs to consider that all this preparation doesn't just happen by itself. I need some help. As her stress escalates, Martha approaches Jesus. "Lord, do you not care that my sister has left me to do all the serving alone? Will you please tell her to help me?"

Martha is startled at Jesus's reply. With wistful eyes and a soft voice, He answers, "Martha, Martha, you are worried and bothered about so many things, but only a few things are necessary, really only one, for Mary has chosen the good part, which shall not be taken away from her."

Martha is speechless. She looks around the room at those who are seated near Jesus. Her eyes then move to the dining room. The table is lovely. She looks at the vase of freshly cut red roses in the center of the white linen tablecloth. Her silver tableware has been polished, the crystal stemware glistens in the candlelight, and her finest dinnerware plates are stacked and ready for serving. Tears well up in her eyes. She wants to retreat privately to a room and deal with her disappointment, but she turns again to Jesus. For the first time, she sees an inexplicable look in His eyes, which quickly melts all the self-pity that she is feeling. She becomes aware of an urgency in His desire to communicate with those who are close to Him. Martha is one of those, and she realizes that she is entirely missing the opportunity.

Jesus continues to teach as Martha settles down near her sister. Eventually, some guests move to the dining room, find the prepared food in the kitchen, and serve themselves. Martha remains seated at the feet of Jesus as she learns about works and discernment from Him.

At some other time, the works I have done today will be good works that His Father will prepare for me to do. Today, they are my works. I overlooked the most important thing: the opportunity to sit at His feet, listen to His words, and have fellowship with Him.

Besides, I have never known Jesus to let people go away hungry. She reflects on a time when Jesus fed a crowd of more than five thousand people. Her thoughts continue, *Even when no preparation was made.*

This was where I ended writing about Martha's day. I felt that I had gotten to know her. Through getting to know her, I got to know myself. It may have been a one-of-a-kind meditation, but it worked for me.

My Response and Prayer

Heavenly Father, while I desire to be more aware and attentive to the needs of others, give me wisdom to discern between my works and the works that You have prepared for me to do. Help me not to overlook the most important thing of all—fellowship with You.

24

A HOUSE NOT LIVED IN

His neighbors knew him as *a good man—a likeable person.* He lived in a small, modest bungalow in a distant city, away from his friends and the place where he had grown up. However, he was a recent heir of a friend who had left his entire estate to him. It was no small sum, to say the least, so he could choose to live anywhere. His choice would be an area that he had read about. He had never actually been there but had once gotten a bird's-eye view when flying over it. He remembered being impressed with the terrain.

This man continued living in a small mediocre bungalow while planning to spend a great portion of his inheritance to build what he called a dream house. Its location was a long flight away from where he currently resided.

Time passed, and finally, the architect's blueprints were

approved, In due time, the foundation was laid, and it was quite a foundation! Because it was a custom-made house, there was no other house like it. He kept going over the plans with his architect/builder and sensed that it was greater and far more elaborate than he had imagined. His enthusiasm grew, and he began writing his friends about his plans. As days and weeks went by, he kept his friends updated on every detail: the size of the master bedroom, each of his many guest bedrooms, which all had adjoining baths, and the view from the wall of windows in the largest of the several entertaining rooms. The magnificent splendor of this house was more than he could accurately describe.

Finally, it was finished, and although he had never taken time to go and see it, he was thrilled with the pictures of the finished house. He wanted to share it with his friends, whom he hoped would eventually come to visit. He kept writing to them and describing its majesty. He even sent pictures. Some of his friends were happy for him. Others became bored with his telling about it but not living in it. He continued to keep them informed as he made plans to move. But the usual and unusual things in life kept him too busy to make the necessary preparations and closure of his current residence and other matters. This included time spent with local friends. Living in his dream house became somewhat of a fantasy that waited for reality. Oh, he kept thinking he would get it all together and would reach the point of finding time to make the move, but life still presented time-consuming delays, both good and not so good.

He didn't mean to stop writing to his friends, but he was so involved in trying to make time to move and thinking it would soon happen that he no longer had time to write them. They never knew that he never moved into that awesome house, which an inheritance had made possible. He had experienced the excitement of seeing the blueprints, and now and then, he saw pictures that helped him visualize the house, but he had not been there. He had not aggressively taken the time and effort to leave what seemed so important to him and move into the grand custom-built home, which was rightfully his to enjoy. But his neighbors and friends remembered him as a good man—one who had a dream.

If Jesus had spoken this as a parable, He would have explained that the *inheritance* is the written Word known as the Holy Bible. The *blueprints* and *pictures* are times that we hear or read the Word and sense the excitement of truth. *The man never moving into his house* is about having good intentions but never seeming to find consistent times to get alone with the Word and sincerely ask and seek God to reveal the grandeur of its meaning.

Here is some food for thought: Is yours a house not lived in—feasibly located on a coffee table, bookshelf, or even a nightstand beside your bed? Do you have good intentions of finding time to make the move? Better yet, are you already experiencing the joy of living in that inherited house whose architect is God? This amazing house is new every morning.

Thy word is a lamp unto my feet, and a light to my path. (Psalm 119:105)

God's word, the Holy Bible, is our inheritance, and there is no other like it.

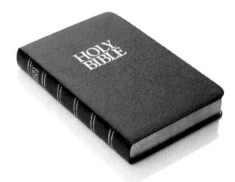

Printed in the United States
by Baker & Taylor Publisher Services